T0154428

HOW TO FIND
THE RIGHT WORDS

HOW TO FIND
THE RIGHT WORDS

The School of Life

Published in 2021 by The School of Life
930 High Road, London, N12 9RT
First published in the USA in 2021
Copyright © The School of Life 2021
Designed and illustrated by Marcia Mihotich
Printed in China by Leo Paper Group

A proportion of this book has appeared online at
www.theschooloflife.com/articles

Every effort has been made to contact the copyright holders of
the material reproduced in this book. If any have been
inadvertently overlooked, the publisher will be pleased to make
restitution at the earliest opportunity.

The School of Life is a resource for helping us understand
ourselves, for improving our relationships, our careers and our
social lives – as well as for helping us find calm and get more
out of our leisure hours. We do this through creating films,
workshops, books, apps and gifts.

www.theschooloflife.com

ISBN 978-1-912891-51-1

10 9 8 7 6 5 4 3

INTRODUCTION

Life constantly presents us with a tension between two very significant forces: we want to let others know how we feel. And we want to be kind. Only too often, the two missions seem entirely opposed. If we revealed the true depths of our anger, frustration, disdain or love, we might ruin a friendship – and end up a pariah in the community. But if we said nothing, we would suffer from a sense of claustrophobia and inauthenticity.

Too often, unsure of how to proceed, we veer between extremes. We say nothing for too long and then, unable to take it any longer, exhausted or at wits' end, we explode. We divulge in an uncontained moment everything that for months we had been too inhibited and cowed to express politely.

We should be generous with ourselves. Speaking up directly but kindly is an art – and we may never have come close to any instruction in how to pull it off (this might even be the first time we're thinking about the matter squarely). Childhood is – as with so many issues – the classroom in which we are likely to have picked up most of what we know about communication and its consequences. Unfortunately, many of us grew up in homes where the art of authentic but gentle transmission was not in evidence. We may have had too many lessons in sulking or screaming, insistence or denial. We may have been exposed to people with such volatile tempers or fragile personalities that we became very 'good' boys and girls. That doesn't mean that we had nothing tricky we wanted to say, but there was just no way that we could dare to say it. We learnt to close our mouths and swallow our complaints. That may still be our first impulse in adulthood – though we now probably also occasionally lapse into the characteristic flipside of the shy and the hyper-polite: what we haven't said for too long emerges in surprising and undignified torrents.

This is a book about diplomacy. Diplomacy is a skill that evolved initially to deal with problems in relationships between countries. The leaders of neighbouring states might be touchy on points of personal pride and quickly roused to anger; if they met head on, they might be liable to infuriate each other and start a disastrous war. So instead, they learnt to send emissaries, people who could state things in less inflammatory ways, who wouldn't take the issues so personally, who could be more patient and emollient. Diplomacy was a way of avoiding the dangers that come from decisions taken in the heat of the moment. In their own palaces, two kings might be thumping the table and calling their rivals by abusive names; but in the quiet negotiating halls, the diplomat would say: 'my master is slightly disconcerted...'

We still associate the term diplomacy with embassies, international relations and high politics but it really refers to a set of skills that matter in many areas of daily life, especially at the office and on the landing, outside the slammed doors of loved ones' bedrooms. Diplomacy is the art of advancing an idea or cause without unnecessarily inflaming passions or unleashing a catastrophe. It involves an understanding of the many facets of human nature that can undermine agreement and stoke conflict, and a commitment to unpicking these with foresight and grace.

Over the coming chapters, we are introduced to a range of scenarios where a lack of diplomacy could be an enormous danger, to our state of mind and to our friendships. Every case requires a slightly different approach but some broad principles of diplomacy can be observed:

The Importance of Respect

The good diplomat remembers, first and foremost, that some of the vehemence with which people insist on having their way draws energy from a sense of not being respected. People will fight with particular tenacity and apparent meanness over so-called small points when they have a sense that the other person has failed to honour their wider need for appreciation and esteem. So diplomatic people put extraordinary emphasis on overall reassurance. Whatever the particular dispute at hand, the diplomat sends out signals that their interlocutor is important, esteemed and completely worthy of their regard. That can make a local complaint so much easier to hear.

Admit Your Own Errors

It helps greatly to know that those making a complaint are not speaking from a position of impregnable perfection but are themselves flawed and aware of the fact. There can be few more successful moves than to confess genially from the outset of a complaint, 'Oh, and I do that all the time myself...'

Massage the Truth

In negotiations, the diplomat is not addicted to indiscriminate or heroic truth telling. They appreciate the legitimate place that minor lies can occupy in the service of greater truths. They know that if certain local facts are emphasised, then the most important principles in a relationship may be forever undermined. Diplomats know that a small lie may have to be the guardian of a big truth. They appreciate their own resistance to the unvarnished facts – and privately hope that others may on occasion, over certain matters, also take the trouble to lie to them, and that they will never know.

Overlook Bad Behaviour

Another trait of the diplomat is to be serene in the face of obviously bad behaviour: a sudden loss of temper, a wild accusation, a very mean remark. They don't take it personally – even when they may be the target of rage. They reach instinctively for reasonable explanations and have clearly in their minds the better moments of a currently frantic but essentially decent person. They know themselves well enough to understand that abandonments of perspective are both hugely normal and usually indicative of nothing much beyond exhaustion or passing despair. They do not aggravate a febrile situation through self-righteousness, which is a symptom of not knowing oneself too well – and of having a very selective memory. The person who bangs a fist on the table or announces extravagant opinions may simply be rather worried, frightened or just very enthusiastic: conditions that should rightly invite sympathy rather than disgust.

Find the Right Moment

The diplomat understands that there are better and worse times to bring up issues. They do not try to get a point across whenever it might first or most apply: they wait till it has the best chance of being heard. That might mean waiting for the morning or for the effects of alcohol to have subsided.

Be Pessimistic

The diplomat's tone of reasonableness is built, fundamentally, on a base of deep pessimism. They know what the human animal is, they understand how many problems are going to beset even a very good friendship, marriage, business or society. Their good-humoured way of greeting problems is a symptom of having swallowed a healthy measure of sadness from the outset. They have given up on the ideal, not out of weakness but out of a mature readiness to see compromise as a necessary requirement for getting by in a radically imperfect world.

Be Frank

The diplomat may be polite, but they are not, for that matter, averse to delivering bits of bad news with frankness. Too often, we seek to preserve our image in the eyes of others by tiptoeing around the harsh decisions – and thereby make things far worse than they need to be. We should say that we're leaving them, that they're fired, that their pet project isn't going ahead, but we mutter instead that we're a little preoccupied at the moment, that we're delighted by their performance and that the project is being actively discussed by the senior team. We mistake leaving some room for hope with kindness. But true niceness does not mean seeming nice, it means helping the people we are going to disappoint to adjust as best they can to reality. By administering a sharp, clean blow, the diplomatic person kills off the torture of hope, accepting the frustration that's likely to come their way: the diplomat is kind enough to let themselves be the target of hate.

* * *

The result of reading this book, and of thereby learning how to find the right words, isn't that we will become consummate liars or well-polished fakes. We will learn how to hit a far narrower but far more valuable target. We will know how to be at once *kind* and *honest*.

I WANT US JUST TO BE FRIENDS

I WANT US JUST TO BE FRIENDS

It is never easy to be rejected but it's arguably a great deal worse to have to reject; the pains of unrequited love are as nothing next to the agonies of having to inflict a dismissal. Someone is willing to offer you everything; concretely, their body, but more metaphysically, their soul, and your answer is in essence a plain: no thank you. But that isn't to say that there aren't far better and worse ways to get the message across. Here's how an ideal note might go:

$\longrightarrow$ *Forgive me for bringing this up...*

It's profoundly tempting to say nothing, to sidestep the interest while the pursuer convinces themselves that you perhaps haven't yet fully noticed or are just profoundly 'shy'. But such ambiguity merely prolongs the torture. You have the agency, maturity and responsibility to bring this to an end.

$\longrightarrow$ *I so love spending time with you...*

The overwhelming priority is to help the rejected candidate preserve their dignity. They aren't a bad or shameful person, they have a huge range of qualities (which is why this is so hard); it's just that sex won't be possible. Be unembarrassed, for embarrassment is catching; if you're not ashamed, they'll have a chance not to be so either. You didn't will your lack of desire, any more than you willed your sexual orientation.

$\longrightarrow$ *... but I feel if we go further...*

Frame the decision as somehow mutual. It isn't simply they who want it and you who conclusively shudders. *We* are looking at this together. Both of you are in theory rather tempted to go forward, you just happen to have noticed a problem from where you're standing.

$\longrightarrow$ *... if we let things develop, you won't get the best out of me.*

It isn't, and can't be, their fault. It's a basic act of kindness to assume responsibility. But, so you must suggest, this has nothing to do with a lack of attraction; it arises from a sincere wish to protect them from your many trickier sides.

$\longrightarrow$ *If this became something else, I'd hate to damage what we have.*

The traditional assumption is that going out with someone gives us access to their best selves: their truest, most authentic and most kindly aspects. But this is plainly false. Most relationships are a calamity of ugliness; we are almost always far better friends than we are lovers. Friendship isn't some kind of consolation prize, it's the truly valuable state besides which the average relationship looks like the squalid alternative.

$\longrightarrow$ *I need your advice, your support and your unique way of looking at the world. Might you be free this Monday to see a show and maybe pick up some supper?*

Make the ongoing offer of friendship concrete. You aren't 'rejecting' them as a whole; you're offering them something far more significant than your sexuality: a chance to enjoy the best sides of you, right now. Friendship is the real gift and privilege.

RELATIONSHIPS

DO YOU STILL LOVE ME?

DO YOU STILL LOVE ME?

Our societies have a lot of patience for people who are in anguish at the start of a relationship because they need to know if they are loved, but a lot less time for those who – deep into established relationships – have an equally powerful longing to know if they are *still* loved. A nagging hunger for reassurance can easily come across as 'needy', 'cloying' or 'desperate'. But that doesn't mean it's illegitimate; it's a wholly normal, even healthy impulse to seek to know where one stands. One just has to find an artful and effective way of doing so.

⟶   *I know this might sound annoying – and no doubt*
    even a touch desperate...

We'll never be overly annoying so long as we're aware we might be so. Giving a mature nod in the direction of the danger suggests that we know the potential for extremes and are determined to avoid them. The truly deranged have no suspicion that they might be so; they just wildly insist on their normalcy.

⟶   *But I need reassurance – and I'm not getting it.*

Too often, when denied a sense of connection, we go down one of two paths. Either we say nothing, avoiding a confrontation out of a sense that we don't deserve good treatment (but then get bitter and go cold or have an affair). Or else we explode into completely uncontained rage, accusing the partner of all manner of extreme things, which makes it painfully easy for us to be ignored and labelled crazy. The trick is to come across as vulnerable and, at the same time, strong.

→ *For me, a sound relationship is about a feeling of*
  connection – and regular communication. I'm
  tough in every area in my life; I don't want to be in
  this one.

A hint should be delivered, somewhere in the message, that while we very much want to stay, we aren't ready to do so at any cost; offering someone unconditional love sounds romantic, but it's also a sure route to getting trampled on.

→ *This might seem like a small thing to bring up, but you*
  need to know that when you .... [insert issue, large or
  substantial: flirted at dinner/were absent for two days
  without saying where you were going/were sullen
  throughout the meal/abandoned your towel on the floor/
  didn't take my hand in bed], it left me sad and a little angry.

We should never be humiliated into feeling that the things that make us unhappy in love are 'too small' to worry about: if they hurt us, they're legitimate. We need to build up our sense that we have every right to speak, which is what will ensure that we can do so with composure.

→ *I love you a lot – but I need to know that we want*
  and deep down feel the same things.

We often don't ask if we're wanted from a bare fear of what we might hear in return. But if a relationship is truly so fragile, we are better off not being in it in the first place.

→ *Of course, I understand that we have different styles*
  of relating; I don't want to put you under undue pressure.

It pays to signal our awareness that love can manifest itself in different ways; it is theoretically compatible with silence, or more modest sexual interest or a steady longing to hang out with friends or play golf. But these may also be signs of a distance that isn't in the end our style and that we have no innate requirement to endure.

$\longrightarrow$ *I'm rather needy – and need a few more signs of life from your end that you care.*

It's useful to win back a pejorative term, make it one's own and triumph over its unfair negative associations. The really fragile ones among us aren't those who can articulate their needs for reassurance, it's those who can't bear the risks of sharing their hunger to be close.

WE SHOULD BREAK UP

WE SHOULD BREAK UP

Normally, the message has been clear in our heads for a very long time. The difficulty isn't so much finding the words; it's coming to terms with the notion that one has the right to say them.

But of course one does – not primarily for our own sake but, far more importantly, for theirs.

⟶   *This is the worst time, I know. But in reality, there*
    simply isn't ever going to be a decent time to say this.

The temptation is to wait until a 'good' moment comes along: when they've settled into their new job, after their birthday, when it's the start of the holidays or when they seem more reliably dissatisfied and annoyed with us. But in reality, whatever date we pick, there never will be a remotely appropriate time. This is going to hurt horribly at any point. One might as well ruin the holiday in Thailand or the brother's birthday in the name of a greater, more sustainable liberation.

⟶   *This relationship simply isn't working for me*
    any more.

The greatest cruelty is not to deliver the blow, but to remain in a relationship one has ceased to believe in without saying anything. The moment one truly realises one's feelings, the primordial duty is to get out of the way – and allow them to start afresh. Wasting someone's life is the real crime.

⟶   *There could be so much to say, but there isn't any*
    point right now. In the kindest way, this is what it is.

The impulse can be to start to go into some of the reasons why. The partner themselves may be particularly intent on taking the conversation in a consultative direction, in the hope of being able to unpick your logic and perhaps reverse your conclusions. But you risk thereby ending up in a petty dispute over a long-standing point of friction or facing a desperate plea – and so having to be blunter than you would wish. If they could understand, properly understand, the real issues, you wouldn't need to be doing this.

$\longrightarrow$ *It may seem like I'm rushing. I'm not. I've thought immensely hard about this – and for a long time too. I'm doing what I know deep down is right.*

The enemy is hope, the feeling that you might be amenable to a change of heart. Truly being nice doesn't mean appearing tender, for this risks being mistaken for the old affection which was so recently available to them. There will be plenty of people to whom the partner will now be able to turn for support. Your job isn't to be delightful, it's to be as forgettable as possible – which means, in essence, to be something of a shit.

$\longrightarrow$ *It's probably best if we're not in touch for a while.*

Brusqueness and artificially constructed insensitivity is, in the circumstances, a gift. It is material with which you can start to become an object of hatred in their eyes – and therefore can be more easily overcome. Generosity involves allowing oneself to be hated. The 'nice person' at the end isn't someone who makes lengthy sensitive speeches and breaks down in hot tears on the way out, it's someone who is brave enough to let themselves be detested by the person they have so grievously injured.

An explanation, in so far as there is one of any kind, should be concise in the extreme.

$\longrightarrow$ *No one is to blame. Ultimately, both of us are better people than we'd ended up being in this relationship. We both deserve better. And one day, years from now, I think you'll agree with me.*

Trying to become friends, or a shoulder to cry on, is only really an option for people who never properly loved each other.

$\longrightarrow$ *The taxi is waiting for me downstairs. Goodbye.*

THERE'S THIS THING ABOUT ME AND SEX

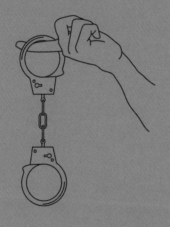

THERE'S THIS THING ABOUT ME AND SEX

There is something you want to try or a fantasy that grips your imagination – a special garment you would like your partner to wear, or a scenario involving another person – but you are worried your partner will find the contents of your mind outlandish or strange. And yet, for the relationship to flourish, you crave for your partner to understand your thought processes. You face a conflict between honesty and kindness.

The immediate tendency is either to remain silent or to stress how much you want something different, which may cast your partner as unadventurous, frightened or disappointing. A better strategy is to shift matters from a demand to a pressure-free, playful, intellectual exploration.

$\longrightarrow$ *I thought both of us could think more about our fantasies as a way of getting to know each other properly. I'd love to understand more about you – and you about me.*

However liberated our societies tell us we are, most of us maintain a deep sense of privacy and shame around aspects of our sexuality. But rather than viewing this as a tragedy, we can turn it into an opportunity to create a unique bond with someone we care for. They will be as unlikely as us to have shared much of who they are sexually.

$\longrightarrow$ *I know this could sound weird, but...*

It's always useful to signal an awareness that one may frighten someone, given that truly weird people never give this a thought.

$\longrightarrow$ *I want to play at being aggressive while obviously loving*

*and caring for you. I want to call you rude and
disrespectful things – even while I profoundly respect you.*

Part of the reason why we feel so ashamed of our desires is that we're
never encouraged to conceive of them as logical. The key move is
to think of every sexual fantasy as counteracting a particular fear or
difficulty in our lives as a whole. Every fantasy tells you fascinating
things about what has been awkward in someone's background.

⟶ *For a long time, I was puzzled why I wanted this. But
then I asked myself: what is this fantasy doing for me?
What bits of my psychology does it appeal to? Given my
past, what fears is it working to alleviate?*

Sexual fantasy isn't usually mysterious; it is a response to a tension
in our lives, which it promises to solve for a while. Someone with
a bad experience around their father might want their partner to
wear a uniform because they wish to re-imagine authority not as
oppressive but as a source of pleasure and reassurance. Someone
might want to play at being submissive because their day-to-day life
places them under almost unbearable pressure to be responsible.

⟶ *When I think about why I might want rough sex, it's
perhaps because the idea counteracts my real experiences
in which I feared that I might hurt those I love by
showing them my more uninhibited sides. It springs from
a longing to be fully myself – and yet acceptable.*

A specific desire has emerged for you because of many precise and
rather touching things about your personal history. What is vital is
to stress that a fantasy is not a plan for real-world action; it is an
alternative to it.

$\longrightarrow$ *I am profoundly uninterested in force in real life. The very idea is shocking. It's just that I love the idea of playing this as a game.*

We adults get confused about games; we often think of them as anticipations of reality. But that is to miss the pleasure of being able to pretend. Children know that you can play at being a wolf or a pirate without wanting to be one in life as a whole; we should be as wise and imaginative.

$\longrightarrow$ *Maybe a lot of us are odder sexually than we suppose; perhaps lots of things are pretty normal that don't sound normal.*

For thousands of generations, being aligned with the standard behaviour of your tribe was an important factor in survival. But our picture of what other people are actually like around sex is liable to be sketchy and distorted. We are all much weirder than we let on – thankfully.

$\longrightarrow$ *I'd love to hear more about the strange-but-actually-not-so strange things that turn you on.*

Intimacy is built on a longing to reveal our 'weirder' sides – and on the joyful discovery that those aspects might be OK with one special person.

YES I DID HAVE AN AFFAIR

YES I DID HAVE AN AFFAIR

Seldom do people feel as certain that they know what's going on in another's head as when they discover that their partner has had an affair. It's seemingly immediately clear why it happened: because the unfaithful partner is mean, deliberately cruel, excessively horny, totally unloving and a profoundly bad person. These beliefs may be true – but they may not be so entirely. The tricky task is to fight back against a set of extremely powerful and socially endorsed assumptions at one of the most raw moments of existence.

$\longrightarrow$ *This is not what you think it is. Truly it isn't...*

What torments the betrayed partner is not so much what happened as what they think it means. The priority is to put forward a different perspective.

$\longrightarrow$ *You'll think it's about sex. It isn't. You'll think I can't love you any more. I do. You'll think I'm only an awful person; heaven knows I've got terrible sides, but might I have others too?*

Strangely, after a time, apologising endlessly may not be the most fruitful move.

$\longrightarrow$ *Obviously I'm so sorry, but if I only ever say sorry, we'll never get beyond this. There are things I need you to understand beyond my guilt and remorse, which are nevertheless (I hasten to add) boundless and deep.*

Though an affair involves sex, it's rarely desire alone that motivates it. The real culprit, almost always, is a feeling of disconnection.

People stray not because they get overwhelmingly lustful, but because they feel disconnected from their partner.

→ *Yes, we had sex, but it wasn't sex that was driving me at heart. I was led by a childish revolt against an appalling feeling that I don't matter to you any more, that we can't get this relationship to work, that we can't get through to one another without shouting or sulks. It was an act of desperation and misplaced anger, not lust.*

You're going to be furious, and you have every right to be, but deep down, what we need to do is somehow reconnect. I need to explain – not right now, but one day – how I feel we grew apart and why the suspicions and the hopelessness started.

I'm not proud of myself, but let me be forensic about where my guilt focuses. I should have been mature enough to address the issues between us directly rather than acting out my distress. I need you to forgive me, not so much for the sex, but for responding so badly and so counter-productively to the distance between us.

As ever, there tends to be a history to this kind of 'acting out'. Childhood has a lot to answer for.

→ *I suppose I grew up unable to believe that I had the right to voice my complaints honestly – and that's why I've acted shiftily, in the shadows and hidden difficult things from you, firstly my disappointments, and then the affair itself.*

But I don't want my past to be my destiny.

Though the temptation is to swear eternal loyalty to the relationship and then to shut up, the need is to get to the issues that powered the infidelity in the first place. That will be the truly noble way to do justice to the crisis.

$\longrightarrow$ *I'll be a penitent as long as you want me to be, I'll*
say sorry as long as you ask me to, but what we really
require to make our relationship work from here isn't – I
feel – guilt alone. It's a chance to address the issues we've
been sweeping under the rug for too long: why we're angry
with each other, how we've disappointed each other, the
resentments we've been harbouring too quietly on each
side. I'm not trying to ignore what's happened, I just
want to address why it happened. And that's not out of
cowardice, it's out of a sincere wish that we don't ever find
ourselves in this position again.

And if we manage to do this, then this affair –
however hurtful and insane it feels right now – might
almost have been a good thing. I want a chance to show
you that I'm not simply a cheating monster. I want to
turn this crisis into an opportunity for us to be as close as
I always longed, but stupidly despaired of knowing how,
to be.

DO YOU WANT TO BE FRIENDS WITH ME?

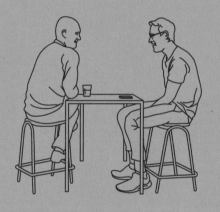

DO YOU WANT TO BE FRIENDS WITH ME?

We hear so much about the tensions and difficulties of asking someone to be our lover, but so little of the challenges of asking someone to be our friend – an equally or arguably even more important request.

$\longrightarrow$ *It was truly such a pleasure to meet and talk.*

Imagine there's someone you've quite recently met who you really rather liked – though not in any romantic sense. It might be hard to state precisely the allure; maybe you were drawn to their sense of mischief or perhaps they said something wise or touching; they might have very neatly defused a potentially tricky social situation or you liked the way they narrowed their eyelids when they were thinking. None of which you could directly say. But you could certainly hint.

$\longrightarrow$ *I'm still laughing about [the story of the dancing dog and the bicycle or of your mother's hat at the wedding] or thinking about [your thoughts on social energy or the atmosphere on Sunday evenings]. I meet so many people, but properly see eye to eye with so few.*

The internal hurdle we may have to overcome is a sense that there is something wrong with us for wanting a new friend. Outside of a few well-established periods – starting college, or on relocating to a new city – it's not readily assumed that decent people might be on the lookout for additions to their social circle. The natural assumption is that if one is remotely interesting, funny, thoughtful or kind, one will already have all the friends one could possibly want. It's hard for us to keep in mind the implausible notion that a person might be both very nice and rather lonely.

$\longrightarrow$ *I wonder if you might want to go out for a meal again at some point.*

The possibility of friendship often stalls because both sides are privately waiting for a sign from the other one as to whether or not they are liked; no one wants to make the first move. Under pressure, we forget the fundamental malleability within the question of whether someone wants to be friends with us or not; in reality, most of it depends on how we behave towards them. Most of us like people who like us; it can be that simple. If we have a little courage and can keep our deep suspicions of ourselves and our terror of their rejection of us at bay, we have every opportunity to turn the situation in our direction.

$\longrightarrow$ *I really liked what you were saying at the end of the evening – and I'm wondering if you could maybe give me a bit of advice; I'm keen to get past a certain mental block I have.*

We might assume that what would make us appealing to someone we like is an aura of being problem-free. However, within reason, offering another person a glimpse of one of our difficulties can be a generous and welcome act, lending them a chance to experience their own competence and intelligence.

$\longrightarrow$ *There's one thing in particular I'd love to talk to you about...*

One of the challenges around establishing a new friendship is that of defining in your own head what the friendship is *for*. The idea that a friendship might have a theme isn't inherently strange but we usually apply it only in quite restricted areas; we understand that someone might be a great companion to go hiking with or an excellent golf partner. But we tend not to extend this useful notion into other potential areas: that we might, for instance, build a friendship around a shared interest in analysing our childhoods or evaluating a city's architecture. There's no shortage of people who are fairly nice; what truly justifies a new friendship is the discovery of delicate and unusual strands of shared perceptions and interests. The sooner we get these clear in our own minds, the more crisply we can hint at what can sustain the union going forward.

$\longrightarrow$ *Perhaps you'd be free one night next week?*

I DON'T WANT TO BE FRIENDS WITH YOU ANYMORE

I DON'T WANT TO BE FRIENDS WITH YOU ANYMORE

In undertaking the quietly momentous task of telling someone that we don't wish to be friends with them anymore, we face a practical and a theoretical hurdle. Strikingly, the practical issue is by far the easiest to address. The central challenge is to accept that we are under no obligation to bow endlessly or limitlessly to the wishes of another person.

A peculiar assumption at large is that good people should never want to prune their social lives. A friend made at one point should remain a friend forever – if one has any virtue or honour. But such a degree of commitment is as implausible as it is ultimately self-defeating. Good friendships need to be sustained by vivid interest on both sides; it is a betrayal of their potential to define them as life-long contracts that cannot be exited without shame.

Imagine a friendship that began a few decades ago. They're very kind, you've had some good laughs together; at one point, you bonded very closely over certain books and the tragi-comic difficulties of dating. But life has moved on: their ideas feel a lot less interesting today and you're in a relationship of your own now.

Crucially, we don't need to think badly of someone to have outgrown them; we can even love a person and for a range of reasons never want to see them again. Wise parents know the importance of not tethering a child too closely to the personality or interests they had at an earlier age; the 14-year-old does not need to be unremittingly true to their 11-year-old predecessor. The same dynamic is in operation at 40 or 80. Friends are not toys or illustrated books but they too are, in part, vehicles for development – and may be respectfully sidestepped when their ongoing presence threatens to impede who we want to become. Wishing to terminate a friendship doesn't have to stem from random infidelity or unfeeling snobbishness: it may simply spring from a sober realisation that we are no longer who we once were.

Part of the problem can be that – out of misplaced guilt – we give out few signs of what is going on inside our minds. The friend may not be unusually deaf, we may be unusually polite – and therefore perplexing to deal with. While railing inside about why we should have to see this person (again), our outward manner may be a picture of geniality; it would take a detective to note that the other was unwanted. We need to have the courage to give voice to our restlessness.

As for the practical aspect, a two-fold move is suggested in response to an enquiry from the friend about whether we might be free to see them at any time in the coming months. Somewhat out of the blue, we might recollect a funny, touching or warm memory that we have of being with them, ideally right at the beginning of the friendship (which might have been many years back).

$\longrightarrow$ *Thanks so much for your email. I was just thinking the other day of that time at university, in our first year, when we took your mother's car out to the beach and sat up all night, chatting about much we hated the course and how lonely we were. I remember that beach hut where we had delicious fried eggs and sweet tea. It was a perfect night. It must have been close to thirty years ago now; how different things are today.*

This rehearsal of a memory serves to remind both of you of why you once became friends. It proves to the other that they have not been forgotten, that very small details still stick in your mind, that they mattered to you. At the same time, this exercise in memory relegates the core of the friendship to a very different time and place. What was truly important happened long ago. Very gently, the message is being imparted that you have developed into quite another person now.

But a little more force is also required. What matters is to keep things short, deliberately mysterious and conclusive. So, in answer to the request for a date at any point in the coming months, one might answer simply:

$\longrightarrow$ *Sadly I'm not going to be able to meet up.*

It's impossible not to hear the message. One clearly isn't angry, nor is one unfeeling. But the decision is evident. None of this is cruel: we are just liberating two people to go out and henceforth do greater justice to the deeper promises of friendship.

I LOVE YOU

I LOVE YOU

It is one of the minor tragedies of social life that we make such rigid and unimaginative distinctions when defining the differences between 'friends' and 'lovers'. When it comes to lovers, one is meant to adore passionately and sexually. With friends, one is meant to love quite a lot but not too much – and, of course, without any sexual intent. And all this is complicated by the powerful Romantic assumption that when we speak of love, we must invariably have physical love in mind.

This is the puzzling and hesitancy-inducing background against which we, at points, experience an intense longing to tell a good friend that we love them. It might be at the end of dinner, as they're recounting a story about their work – and we're suddenly overwhelmed by a sense of how interesting, decent and amusing they are. Or we might be on a trip, flying high above Greenland, and we randomly start to think of how much we miss them and what an interesting time we would have if we could be talking to them right now.

But unfortunately, the structure of friendship does not generally allow a message of love to be imparted; the declaration risks being read as a prelude to an unwanted physical advance (perhaps they are married or of another orientation). Or it might feel overwhelming and intense, as though – once such a declaration had been made – there would be no alternative but to move in with them and cling to them tightly.

To counteract such fears, we should begin with a basic realisation: hearing from someone that you already hold in high esteem and feel fond of that they love you is one of the most pleasant occurrences possible in an otherwise alien and disappointing world. Intense it may be; dreadful it can't be.

$\longrightarrow$ *I know this might sound very silly – and a bit embarrassing too...*

It never hurts to let out a few indications that we won't, whatever happens, be asking them to tuck us in tonight (or only if they want to).

$\longrightarrow$ *...but I was just thinking of how much you mean to me.*

One of the basic mysteries of friendship is that we can't easily tell how much our friend might think of us when we're not around. But if we judge the matter by how much we think of them, then it's fair to assume the same is happening in the other direction too. This is a touching and sweet realisation, and one that should give us confidence to carry on.

$\longrightarrow$ *I often find myself thinking of you: your advice, your perspectives, your sense of humour – all of these matter so much to me.*

Another mystery we labour under is where we are placed in our friends' hierarchy of affection: is one in their top twenty, or top ten best friends? Does one make the top eight? Even five? Outside of closed circles like schools and universities, we don't know the full range of anyone's friendship groups and therefore where we might fit in. Touchingly, we're also often in the position of fearing that we're far lower down the pecking order than we in fact are; few of us have a secure sense of our worth.

$\longrightarrow$ *I have a lot of friends, but I don't have many like you. You're one of three friends I care about most in the entire world.*

Why wait until a fatal diagnosis to express such intimate treasures?

$\longrightarrow$ *I know we don't see each other too often – it's ridiculous how much life gets in the way – but that's no reflection of the space you occupy in my heart.*

None of this is a romantic declaration. It's something far more significant. The Ancient Greeks, wiser than us in so many fields, had two words for love: *eros* to describe sexual attraction, and *philia* to capture the feeling of a person being an immensely close soulmate. We may not 'love' our friend in the standard way, but we love them far more richly and sensitively than that: as our long-lost Platonic other half.

$\longrightarrow$ *I had this rather nice dream the other night. You and I were walking around an amazing city, like a cross between Venice and Berlin. It's impossible to capture what it was like, but it felt exciting that we were exploring it together.*

I know we'll be seeing each other soon. I was thinking of asking another friend to join us, but then I thought it might be nicer if it was just the two of us.

I CAN'T TAKE YOUR SUCCESS

I CAN'T TAKE YOUR SUCCESS

When your friendship began, your situations were similar; you were both studying or taking the early, uncertain steps in your careers; your hopes and anxieties didn't look too different; you lamented the foibles of your respective bosses; you went on holiday together for a week and had a great time staying in a run-down hotel and searching out places you could eat in for almost nothing.

But for a while things have been going strikingly well for your friend around work. They don't go on about their success but it keeps on being evident: they invite you to their house-warming party and their new apartment is conspicuously elegant; they ask your advice about a presentation they're giving – and it's obviously at a much more impressive conference than any you'd be asked to. Instead of feeling pleased for them you resent their success. Thinking of them makes you feel your life has stalled; in a dark – but insistent – part of your mind you secretly wish they could get the sack or discover that their partner was having an affair.

There's plenty you still like about this person but it's swamped by your feelings about their success. If you don't resolve this, you'll drift apart. But even if you never see them again, they'll still haunt your imagination.

It's probably not going to help if you dramatically confront them with a candid statement of your resentment. It's not that you want to make them painfully aware that their success disturbs you: there isn't much they can do with this information, except feel very sorry that this difficulty has emerged between you. They didn't build their success in order to humiliate you.

But there are some more oblique strategies that could help.

$\longrightarrow$ *I've been feeling rather frustrated with my own*

progress – I think it's partly prompted by seeing how
amazingly you've been getting on.

We tend to assume that only we could possibly perceive our own envy – and that others will be in the dark. But envy is one of the most transparent of all emotions. Rather than wait for it to be discovered, better to name it oneself, suggest that one has some distance from it – and gain a victory over the shame.

$\longrightarrow$ *As you can imagine, I've been kicking myself – and*
going quietly green. But that's ridiculous, I know. I
wonder if there's something I should be doing that I'm not
seeing? If you were in my shoes, what do you think you
might do?

A key to dealing with envy is to realise that one doesn't really want someone else's life; one just wants to make a few strategic changes to one's own. Instead of trying to repress our envy, we should henceforth make every effort to study it. Each person we envy possesses a piece of the jigsaw puzzle depicting our possible future. There is a portrait of a 'true self' waiting to be assembled out of our envious pangs. We should calmly ask one essential and redemptive question of all those we envy: 'What could I learn about here?'

$\longrightarrow$ *I've been thinking quite a lot about envy recently:*
maybe it's one of those things we all feel. But I'm curious:
who do you feel envious of?

Because every life is incomplete, it is entirely logical that your friend must feel envy too. Without being dark or cruel, it's helpful to hear who they might be envious of: it restores a degree of equality and might even remind you that there are people who will right now be envying you.

$\longrightarrow$ *I'd be fascinated to hear about the kinds of difficulty you face with the work you're doing. I imagine it's a bit like climbing a mountain; the higher up you get, the harder it becomes.*

You're getting them to share the less appealing aspects of their success (you can all too easily imagine the nice aspects): the risks, the pressure, the fact that nothing is ever quite enough. Another person's life – however burnished it might appear on the outside – is sure to contain a full measure of confusion, worry, conflict, disappointment and self-criticism. It's not gossipy or mean to want to understand how things truly are for others ahead of us. If we can get to understand what's not so good about their lives, we can get a better perspective on our own situation. We're not making a fair comparison when we see all the troubles of our own life but only the external accomplishments of theirs. We might – strangely – have a number of things to feel very grateful for.

THANK YOU FOR DINNER

THANK YOU FOR DINNER

Life continually requires that we write down a few words of thanks: for holidays, meals, presents or parties. However, too often, our messages end up flat or unconvincing; we say that the dinner was 'nice', the present 'brilliant' and the holiday 'the best ever', all of which may be true while failing to get at what truly touched or moved us.

To render our messages more effective, we should take a lesson from an unexpected quarter: the history of art. Many paintings and poems are, in effect, a series of thank you notes to parts of the world. They are thank yous for the sunset in springtime, a river valley at dawn, the last days of autumn or the face of a loved one. What distinguishes great from mediocre art is the level of detail with which the world has been studied. A talented artist is, first and foremost, someone who takes us into the specifics of the reasons why an experience or place felt valuable. They don't merely tell us that spring is 'nice', they zero in on the particular contributing factors to this niceness: leaves that have the softness of a newborn's hands, the contrast between a warm sun and a sharp breeze, the plaintive cry of baby blackbirds.

The more an artist moves from generalities to specifics, the more the scene comes alive in our minds. A great painter goes beneath a general impression of pleasure in order to select and emphasise the truly attractive features of the landscape: they show the sunlight filtering through the leaves of the trees and reflecting off of a pool of water in the road; they draw attention to the craggy upper slopes of a mountain or the way a sequence of ridges and valleys opens up in the distance. They've asked themselves with unusual rigour what it is that they particularly appreciated about a scene and faithfully transcribed their most salient impressions.

An effective thank you note might have some of the

following ingredients:

$\longrightarrow$ *i. A determination to break clichés*
You are both so close to my heart. Too often when I go out,
I get bored, return home, take off my socks and wonder
what it was all about – and why we make such efforts
for nothing. But that was the literal opposite of what I
experienced on returning from your house.

$\longrightarrow$ *ii. A little hyperbole*
You did nothing less than rekindle my enthusiasm for
humanity.

$\longrightarrow$ *iii. Colour*
And in the company of one of the best paellas I've ever
tasted and some of the liveliest and kindest people one
could hope to meet.

$\longrightarrow$ *iv. Details*
It's the stickiness of the rice that normally lets everything
down. But yours was substantial, sweet and tangy
without being overwhelming; and adding that touch of
crab was so deft and bold.

$\longrightarrow$ *v. Discoveries*
You were properly thoughtful to put me next to someone
who had such an original take on things – and managed
to tease me about my shoes as well (she was right!).

$\longrightarrow$ *vi. Brevity & intensity*
I know how much work goes into an evening like that.
You're the epitome of grace and kindness. I love you – and

want to see more of you very soon.

Praise works best the more specific it can be. We know this in love; the more a partner can say what it is they appreciate about us, the more real their affection will feel.

The person who has given a dinner party or sent us a present is no different. They too hunger for praise in its specific rather than general forms. We don't have to be great artists to send effective thank you notes: we just need to locate and hold on tightly to two or three highly detailed reasons for our gratitude.

I'VE SCREWED UP

I'VE SCREWED UP

One of the greatest problems of our working lives is that we lack any experience of, or instruction in, the essential art of failing well. Because our efforts are focused on appearing utterly professional and flawless, because we are guided by an underlying and punishing notion that we might avoid failure altogether, we lack the energy or insight to respond productively to our inevitable stumbles. We forget an essential truth: the issue at work is never whether we will fail or not; simply whether we will fail well or not.

Our bad failures tend to follow a familiar pattern: we deny that anything has gone, or could even go, wrong. When conclusively rumbled, we deny there is much of an issue, blame the person who upbraids us, and suggest they might be being absurdly mean or critical. Or else we fold and go in for histrionic apology, beg for our lives, overdo the contrition and make our colleagues wish they had never said anything to begin with.

A wiser response to screwing up might have some of the following components:

$\longrightarrow$ *i. A clear and unashamed sorry*
I'm going to put my hands up here. I've made a mistake.
I'm so sorry.

Half of the population at least is trapped in defensive – perfectionist patterns of behaviour. That is, they suffer from an extreme reluctance to acknowledge fault and, when it's pointed out to them, imagine that their entire selves are under assault, as opposed to trusting that it is merely one of their behaviours that is being critiqued. They are told it would be great if they could increase the margin size on a document. All they can hear is 'You don't deserve to exist'. One tells them it would have been great if the August figures had been a bit higher; they assume you want them dead. A prerequisite of a good apology is therefore a sound sense of self. You can fail and still have every right to walk the earth.

⟶   *ii. A technical explanation for the screw-up*
      One reason I messed up was because the systems I'm
      working with meant that...

There is almost always, at some level, a *technical* reason for an error. It pays for everyone to know what this might be – so that corrections can be put in place. Which indicates that there is only one thing the senior management ever really cares about when it comes to mistakes: that things can go better going forward. There is complete uninterest in poring over the entrails of the failure – *except in so far as this can help with the future.* Our task is to draw attention to every clue that will help them in this regard.

⟶   *iii. An emotional explanation for the screw-up*
      If I can be frank for a moment, there's a lot going on at
      home which means I might not have been in the best
      frame of mind.

We too often enter the workforce with the punishing idea that to be a good employee means being an emotionless automaton, and therefore that having to admit to emotional disruptions is tantamount to declaring oneself unemployable. But our terror stems from a misunderstanding. The good-enough employee isn't the one who never endures some emotional static, it's the one who can get a perspective on their fragilities and can be honest about their difficulties from a background appreciation of their many genuine strengths.

Companies never set out to replace people; they want to

develop the ones they have – and so what they crave is a hopeful narrative of why they should keep faith with those already in their posts. That means, in essence, that they long for employees to show what exactly they have learnt from each of their mistakes.

$\longrightarrow$ *iv. Evidence of lessons drawn*
What I'm going to take away from this incident is
three things in particular. Firstly..., secondly..., thirdly...

$\longrightarrow$ *v. A capacity to move on*
Now for the meeting next week...

It's distinctly possible to apologise *too much*. If we plead for forgiveness, insist we are the world's greatest idiot or swear never to make the slightest mistake ever again, it suggests we don't have a clear sense of the reality of the situation. Our tears don't bring back lost profit and our promises sound untrue. The most useful thing we can do, to express our maturity and competence, is to get back to our desk, remain confident and work with ever greater astuteness.

THERE'S SOMETHING WRONG WITH YOU

THERE'S SOMETHING WRONG WITH YOU

We tend to have a pretty confident attitude towards the *technical* failings of the people we work with. These failings may be maddening, but we know how to put them right: someone needs to go on a course to update their knowledge of building regulations or attend a seminar on data entry. We don't feel too much angst around pointing out either the problem or the remedy.

But it's entirely different when it comes to an equally serious range of failings a colleague might have in psychological, temperamental or personal areas. It feels much harder – weird, 'heavy' and impossible – to mention that they go on too much in meetings; that they use too much (or not enough) deodorant; that they appear too posh when dealing with clients; that they come across as petty and pedantic; or that they seem rather defensive in the face of even mild criticism. These are matters we could raise with our partner or perhaps a close friend but at work, to do so seems to overstep an unwritten but very real boundary.

The core task is to let another person know of their issue in a way that makes them trust that they have not simply meanly been singled out for fruitless cruel condemnation. And there is no better way to help them do this than to manifest a frequent mature and genial recognition of our own flaws of character.

$\longrightarrow$ *Yet again, I was a bit of an idiot last week. While trying to get a point across to some clients, I managed to get unnecessarily fired up. I guess I felt criticised and under pressure and, in a defensive mood, made claims that I don't actually believe in. Of course, no one directly mentioned anything at the time, but I could see that they kept looking at me in this strange way. I'm going to need to think about all that.*

Or

*I'm having a lot of angst around X, they're so
intimidating – at least to me – I find myself mumbling
and just agreeing with them like I've got no mind of
my own. I'm going to have to do something about it –
but what?*

*Oh by the way, speaking of my trouble, I was just
wondering...*

The tendency to defensiveness is set off not just because a statement feels critical but because we assume that we could not both have a given failing and be understood and thought a decent person. So a central move – prior to breaking news to a colleague – is to establish your own position as a fellow and repeated sufferer. You're not saying you have their flaw precisely, just one of similar gravity and worthy of a similar quota of embarrassment, but then also of plentiful doses of forgiveness and understanding. Your own failing must be current, rather than be consigned to an earlier phase of existence (it is crushing to be told 'I used to have your problem' which at once implies an enraging superiority). And it helps if it seems as though you are at once aware of the problem and still actively searching for a way forward.

$\longrightarrow$ *Whenever someone criticises me, I always have a
habit of thinking: 'that can't be true, you're just being
mean'. I know people say not to take it personally but I'm
struggling with trying to remember that at key
moments...*

Or

I have such trouble choosing the right sort of clothes in the morning. I want to look smart – I guess we all do – but I also want to remain comfortable. I know sometimes I get it a bit wrong and maybe come across as scruffy, even just messy. I wonder if you've ever felt like that?

All our personal failings are essentially inadvertent. Most people don't say anything to us about them not because these failings don't exist, but because they don't care about us enough to undertake the emotional effort that is required to mention them. None of us needs a huge lecture to take on board what is being said. The most mild wink in the direction of the matter will almost always be enough for a lifetime. We may even eventually realise that we've not been singled out for mockery; we've been given a gift.

In the ideal office there would be a notice hanging above the door saying: *Everyone here has an awkward personal failing. Except me: I have many.*

DID YOU HAVE A NICE WEEKEND?

DID YOU HAVE A NICE WEEKEND?

Some of what makes office life awkward is that it asks us to tread a fine line between being, on the one hand, efficient and focused and, on the other, genial and human. We mustn't appear robotic, but nor should we gush naively in a boundary-less way. This is especially important in relation to a number of stock enquiries that we are likely to face, one of the most inevitable of which is: *Did you have a nice weekend?* How we handle such a question is a minor but key indicator of how well we have made our peace with the delicate compromises and hypocrisies of professional existence.

On the surface, this is exactly the kind of question that you could be asked by a close friend – or your psychotherapist. Chatting in a café, or lying on the couch, you might explain that things were not going well with your partner. The painful issue is that you're not having much sex any more. This has been leading to a lot of arguments. On Saturday morning, feeling rejected, you picked a fight about how dirty the kitchen was, focusing on the fridge especially. That meant your partner was resentful about needing to see your friends from Canada in the evening. By Sunday afternoon, you were rethinking your whole relationship, questioning your career, doubting what happened to you in your childhood and wondering whether life was essentially a cruel joke. You also had a stomach upset because of a prawn sandwich you had at lunch on the Sunday. And how was *your* weekend?

Evidently, if you were to launch into such a rendition at 9.03am with your colleague from sales, you would soon overstep the limits of their curiosity and good will and be marked down as a garrulous, naive, frightening, depressive egotist. Being professional means, willingly denying the complexities of being human.

One response to the tension between the sincere and the professional is to treat small talk with disdain and give almost nothing away. In response to your enquiry about the weekend, you might look at your colleague as if they had said something inappropriate and enquire, with a cold degree of puzzlement: 'why do you ask?' Being inquisitive about a colleague's weekend could be framed as a species of sinister curiosity, as if a police officer had asked what you'd been up to on your Saturday afternoon.

Office life makes some peculiar demands of us. We cannot be properly ourselves, but nor can we be entirely faceless either. We are likely to be part of a group of almost random strangers of varied ages and backgrounds who have been temporarily aligned in the pursuit of money. But we are, nevertheless, called upon to treat each other with tolerance, kindness and empathy. We are meant both to care and not really to care. This is a dance, and a taxing one for those among us who prize sincerity and authenticity. What is going on in someone's inner world, how their new puppy is, or the state of their relationship is not relevant to anything on the agenda – and yet, because these belong to the reality of the participants, nor are they irrelevant either. They need to be touched, but not settled, on.

The question about what sort of weekend a colleague had is not purely fake: the asker isn't just complying with a convention that they regard as ridiculous; they do want to know something. Calibrating the answer well emerges from an understanding of the point of the question.

Your colleague isn't keen to know the details of your life outside the office. But just below the surface, small talk performs an important function. It is a tool of orientation. It allows the bare bones of another's situation to emerge, so that – were it to be necessary – one would know who to call in an emergency and what guesses to make about someone's behaviour. It allows for a rough estimate of character; it tells us how attuned someone might be to group dynamics; how they might react in a crisis, and how competitive or trustworthy they might prove. Not least, both the raising and the answering of small talk signals a mutual commitment to civility within the otherwise chilly bounds of commercial life.

$\longrightarrow$ *Pretty good; I was down on the water with some friends.*
Lovely to get away from it all. And you?

Modern capitalism has moved work in two contradictory directions. On the one hand, it has made it evident that we are individuals competing for economic survival in a ruthless and unforgiving environment; on the other hand, it has identified that the psychological well-being and mental health of employees has a minor but critical role to play in the success of every firm.

We should not resent our colleagues for not being our friends, but nor should we make the mistake of thinking that they are. We should forgive the world of work for placing us at a tantalising midpoint between the human and the instrumental.

$\longrightarrow$ *Do you think you'll be doing anything nice next*
weekend?

DO IT NOW!

DO IT NOW!

A deadline is looming and a member of your team hasn't made much progress on the crucial part of the task that's been assigned to them. You feel like going up to them and insisting they make a concentrated effort immediately: *Do it now!* The strong temptation is to get stern and controlling – and keep them at it, under your eye if need be, until it's finished.

But there's a huge problem: your peremptory demands are very likely to undermine your colleague's ability to perform. They'll feel flustered and harassed; they'll not be able to muster the necessary levels of attention and energy; they'll make mistakes. Just as significantly, they'll get resentful: they'll begin to see you as a tyrant to be hated rather than a team member to be helped.

The more work requires the use of the mind, the more galling the situation becomes. It's possible (at a theoretical extreme) to make someone hew rocks or chop trees more or less at gunpoint. People who ran slave galleys didn't have to worry about team morale. For thousands of years, the only tool of management was the whip. But it's not nowadays remotely possible to motivate an unhappy employee to identify an anomaly in the year-end accounts or come up with a resonant ad slogan or make an elegant refinement to a dress design by being mean and impatient. The more worried, oppressed or anxious an individual feels, the less likely it is that the creative and delicate elements of their mind will ever be coaxed into action. You might be able theoretically to browbeat them into getting the job done – but it won't be work you'll ever have any use for.

$\longrightarrow$ *I'm so sorry to contact you; I know I must come across as deeply annoying and unreasonable. However, I'm just wondering how you might be getting on with*

*the project. Your work is so valuable, we need you more
perhaps than you can realise. I might just be fretting,
and maybe you have it all in hand, but if you could try to
make sure that you can meet (ideally comfortably!) the
deadline we agreed, I for one will feel so much more at
ease. Needless to say, I'm simply so grateful – and deeply
look forward to hearing from you whenever time allows.*

The strategy and vocabulary originate in a place that doesn't immediately seem to have any connection to the modern office: international diplomacy. Diplomacy emerged as the urgently needed alternative to the devastations of war; if you could soothe and encourage, rather than insist, it might be possible to avoid besieged cities and bodies on the field. Diplomacy turned to words like 'possibly', 'maybe' and 'perhaps' in order to create space for the free (rather than enforced) assent of the other. It used praise rather than criticism and suggestion rather than a hectoring demand. It wasn't the result of cowardice or weakness, but of a painfully learned lesson in the way in which a just cause, directly stated, can completely fail to get the desired results.

In our panic, we tend to get stern and forget what we know from the inside. We ourselves don't respond well to being badgered. Instead it's the feeling that we are loved, valued, appreciated and liked that brings out the best in our cognitive capacities and builds our motivation: we feel safe enough to explore a promising but difficult line of thought; we feel encouraged to do the absolute best we can; we get more imaginative, more perceptive and more energetic.

We're encountering the work version of a large – and maddeningly central – feature of the human condition: the correctness and legitimacy of a message doesn't immediately get the person who hears it to do the reasonable or right thing.

A sarcastic demolition of an absurd idea tends to entrench

those who believe it; proving by facts and logic that someone is an idiot usually does little to induce them to be reasonable and wise. If you insist that your child eats some lettuce because 'nutritionists have proved it will help with cardiovascular circulation and you won't get any screen time if you don't,' they will be sure to develop a lifelong aversion to greens; if a teacher is openly appalled that a pupil fails to understand something, their chances of remedying the error are massively reduced. When environmental activists make us feel hopeless, sinful and guilty, we tend to turn away and pretend there is no problem with our planet.

$\longrightarrow$ *I shouldn't worry, I know, you do amazing things at this company; but if there's any way you might let me know whether the project is progressing as it should, then you'd be able to put my fears finally and fully to rest. I know that, as always, you'll be able to do such a brilliant job.*

It may feel like another frantic Thursday afternoon but in fact you are participating in an honourable and eternal struggle: to make a difficult truth powerful and attractive in the complex mind of another person.

YOU'RE FIRED

YOU'RE FIRED

Some things are awkward to say not so much because they require a particularly deft or careful choice of words, but because it's difficult to get into the frame of mind in which we feel it's legitimate for us to say what we have to say.

It's so hard to tell someone that they're fired because we want to see ourselves as good people. And to get to grips with the difficulty of firing someone we have to ask an important – but usually ignored – question: 'what is it to be good?'

Mostly we don't ask because the answer already feels obvious: being good involves making other people happy; it means being nice and being warm and generous towards the hopes and feelings of the people around us. This answer is endlessly reinforced from childhood on; in all children's books when a mean character learns to be good, it's because they start paying more attention to the concerns of other people. They discover empathy, compassion and tenderness.

This is why firing someone makes us feel so awful: we're acutely aware that being dismissed will distress them; they'll feel humiliated; they might weep; they might get angry and tell us that we don't care about them at all and that we're treating them in a monstrously unfair way.

But there's another model of goodness, which is very important in our practical lives – but which doesn't get nearly as much attention. This is the idea of goodness-as-excellence. Someone is a good tennis player because of the reliable, superlative ('excellent') accuracy with which they play their shots; they may not have particularly tender or sweet thoughts about their opponents. In fact, at times, victory will mean that their opponents are going to be frustrated, disappointed, even infuriated. The good tennis player isn't setting out to humiliate, they aren't randomly cruel, it's just that on the court, their eye is on something else besides niceness: playing the game really, really well.

The divergence between goodness-as-niceness and goodness -as-excellence sometimes comes to a head when selecting people for teams. There may be a child who has set their heart on being in the school swimming team; they practice a lot and they're good friends with others already in the squad. But if they're not a properly good swimmer they can't and shouldn't get a place on the squad, even when their friend is choosing. They're being rejected not out of cruel indifference to their feelings but out of a devotion to excellence.

And it's the same thing that happens around firing someone. They have to be fired not because they have a bad soul, but because they are not good at their job. The person who fires them is being good, just not in the good-as-niceness way: they are showing an honourable devotion to the excellence of a business.

Part of the pain of being a boss is that you can't be sentimental; in other words, you can't aim for two incompatible things and then avoid making a choice. Society on the whole is sentimental in a number of areas – people who, for instance, will happily eat a chicken sandwich will recoil in horror from the sight of an industrial slaughterhouse. We want companies to provide good products and services at a decent price, but we don't like the idea of people being fired from their jobs. To be a boss is, in effect, to have to run the slaughterhouse as well as the sandwich shop. It means having to do the things that are not at all nice in the service of the good.

The actual words of the meeting might be fairly simple, quick and direct (it's like ripping off a sticking plaster in one painful moment rather than prolonging the agony by teasing it off gradually):

→   *I'm so sorry but we're going to have to let you go. We all respect and like you hugely. But the needs of our team are taking us in a new direction. I know this is very painful – but I do hope that one day, not now but one day, you'll realise that this truly isn't personal.*

The hard thing isn't stringing the words together, it's realising that in saying them you are not, as you fear, being a conclusively horrible person; you're following a lonely, but genuine, path to a distinctive kind of goodness.

I'M SO SORRY FOR LETTING YOU DOWN

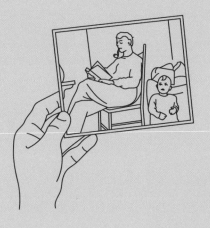

I'M SO SORRY FOR LETTING YOU DOWN

There are few things more appalling for the parent of a grown-up child than the realisation of just how much one has, over the years, deeply hurt the person one most loves in the world – and has done so out of nothing more noble than stress, self-absorption and profound stupidity. To compound the agony, children are not – by nature – inclined to extend time or complex sympathy towards their flawed parents; they need them to have been there at the start, and to have been sane, kind and gentle, and can't be expected to search too deeply for reasons why they weren't. It is normal to move on, take the hurt elsewhere and bristle at any cack-handed parental attempts at reconciliation.

Still, you may not be able to leave it at that. Something inside you may crave a chance to speak at greater length:

$\longrightarrow$ *Forgive me for interrupting you; I know you're hugely busy at the moment. I'm so proud of you for everything that you do.*

I just wanted to say a few words about some of the things that we never get around to discussing, but that are always on my mind; about some of the difficulties that went on between us and in the family more broadly when you were younger – and that I feel desperately sorry about, more than I will ever really properly be able to say. I'm speaking not with any expectation that things can change, but just to let you know how much regret I carry, how much I love you and care for you – and how much I want you to feel free and unburdened.

It must be hard for you to imagine perhaps, but

*your mother/father and I were so young – at least
psychologically – when you were little. There was so much
we didn't understand – about ourselves and about one
another. We both had complicated pasts that made us
less than ideally suited to be together. We got impatient
and intolerant. We didn't know how to find the words to
tell each other difficult stuff. A lot got buried and then
came out in very wrong ways. We tried hard not to let
things impact you, but ultimately and evidently not hard
enough. There were things you heard and saw that I'm
agonised about; it wasn't fair – ever – to put you in that
sort of situation. Bringing you into the world was the
finest thing that your mother/father and I ever did.*

*Work didn't make things any easier. It must also be hard
for you to imagine just how rocky things were in those
days. I had to put in so many more hours than I would
have wanted. Sometimes whole weeks went by without
me being able to properly connect with the family. I
don't expect you to understand, let alone forgive me.
There could have been other ways to arrange my life,
I know; other people find it after all, but I couldn't. I
lacked imagination, I was stubborn and scared – and
overwhelmed by a rigid sense of duty – which meant that
the people I was doing all this for suffered far more than
they should.*

*When it came to your education, I lacked imagination.
I think I must have conveyed the impression that I was
obsessed with your results – but I didn't care as much
as I implied. I was just worried, and my fretting came
to find a home in a blunt way around school. Truly the*

only thing that matters to me is your happiness, it's what I always felt – but was too narrow-minded properly to recognise and articulate.

It isn't your business to understand all this. I just want you to know that I'm the proudest parent in the world. I'm also a deeply flawed one – and you've every right to feel as you do. What I need you to know now is just how much I'm aware of things, and how committed I am to making them better in any way I can – even if that means shutting up and leaving you to it.

I never want you to come and see me out of duty, only when you want and when it feels completely right. I am always here for you; I love you so much.

Your child will perhaps never (and perhaps never should) understand entirely – and therefore see you as just an ordinary person afflicted with the usual range of human weaknesses and prone to the normal, deep mistakes of existence. They won't ever be fair to you. And that's fine. But the two of you can maybe be closer, much closer, if you dare to speak.

I'M ANGRY

I'M ANGRY

One of the more shocking and difficult emotions one may feel towards one's parents is anger. It might have been acceptable, as a toddler, to have had the odd tantrum in front of them or even to have been a bit sulky as a teenager, but as an adult, one is meant to have developed a broadly benevolent and friendly relationship to them. Society keeps enforcing the message by presenting us with situations where one should be keen to get together: holidays, birthdays and the inevitable Mother's and Father's Days. But for some of us, these demands are intensely oppressive. We cannot smile as we should. We can't write the card that so-called normal people would write. Our manner is strained around the parental dinner table. We can't wait to head back to our lives. We find aspects of chatting to them unbearable. We know our parents love us and, despite everything, we love them too. But their company is in a practical sense truly untenable. We feel at once guilty and oppressed. We call far less than we should. We'll feel devastated but also not a little relieved on the terrible day when they'll no longer be around.

Might there be a way of clearing the atmosphere? We probably long – deep down – to have it out with them and explain more about our avoidant manner, whose roots lie in childhood. Instead of sending them the usual meaningless cheery postcard, might we not – for once – try to speak the awkward truth to them? It can take a very long time to be clear in our own minds about our feelings – and to develop the courage to speak.

→   *Dear Mum and Dad,*
       I know this could sound like a very weird message. I've
       often thought of sending you something like this – and
       then stopped myself. Partly that's because I love you so

much and would hate to cause you hurt and upset. And partly (and I know this could strike you as odd) because I'm somewhere inside still a little scared of you.

The range of possible complaints is broad. Some of the following might be relevant:

$\longrightarrow$ *I know how much I must have disappointed you at times. But the process went both ways. At many levels, you provided me with everything I needed. There are so many children who had it far worse. But sometimes I craved things nevertheless: simple acceptance, raw affection, a feeling that I mattered – truly mattered – to you. You tell me often enough now that you love me, and I'm so touched that you do, but there were gaps back then, times when that wasn't at all what it felt like and I carry the legacy of that to this day. Without me meaning for this to be, there's a part of me that rages against you still – even though all I want to do is love you.*

I know that you didn't mean any of what went on – but it marked me profoundly. It's made me less than I should be. It's affected my relationships and my work. I try not to burden you with this, but I wrestle with the past more than I should.

I don't want to be angry; I want to be close to you and to love you without inhibition. I want nothing more than for our family to be at ease. I am dutiful, perhaps too dutiful. But if all I ever am is dutiful, then my feelings will be fake or strained. I need to let out a little howl, I need to be properly myself with you – and to see that you can take that side of me, so that later my affection can be as warm as it should be.

Don't think me too mad, or eccentric. What matters is that I love you, that I am doing this because I care – and in the hope that we can in the years ahead be as happy around one another as can be.

Even though all this might be addressed to them, you're not – fortunately – doing it for their sake, you're doing it for yours: as a sign of maturity, and evidence to yourself that you aren't scared any more in relation to the errors of the past. It's a demonstration that you have found a voice. You cannot lose. Either they will understand – and you will be closer. Or they won't understand – and you will be free.

I LOVE YOU BUT WE HAVE
SO LITTLE IN COMMON

I LOVE YOU BUT WE HAVE SO LITTLE IN COMMON

Generally we select our companions and friends on the basis that we have a lot in common with them. We enjoy the same activities, we have broadly the same values, we share a sense of humour or we enjoy discussing the same topics.

But the central feature of families is that we don't choose who we are related to. Looking round a family gathering we might be struck by the thought that there isn't a single person here that we'd spend time with, if it didn't happen to be for the accidents of genetics and matrimony.

There's a younger cousin who is very shy and keen on tap-dancing and obsessed with a video game we've hardly heard of. There's an aunt who is rather bossy and fussy and who tells long stories about bridge competitions. There's a brother-in-law who is a very decent person, but whose outlook, temperament and interests are very different from our own. And our sister, perhaps, has political views our friends would find disturbing and often quotes approvingly a newspaper we'd only refer to for comic effect.

But these people are still important to us. We built sandcastles on the beach with our sister when we were four; there's an intonation in her voice, when she says certain words, that's precisely – and uniquely – the same as ours; the younger cousin's nose is just like that of the grandmother we share; the bridge-playing aunt was very kind when we were small, and gave us a brown velvet monkey who lived under our pillow for years; the brother-in-law has been deeply helpful in sorting out our mother's finances. For some of them, we will attend their funerals; some of them will be there at ours.

It's not an exaggeration to say that we love these people. But often, when we're together we resort to discussing innocuous things: it was unexpectedly nice weather yesterday, the roads weren't too busy getting here.

A way we can express our love is through asking them about the things that interest them – even if the overt topic isn't one that's directly of interest to us.

$\longrightarrow$ *I forget what age you would have been when you started learning to tap-dance? Who did you learn with? Were they a good teacher? What was tricky to learn?*

Has your attitude to bridge changed over the years? Who do you particularly enjoy playing with? What makes them a good partner or opponent?

What was my mother / father like when they were fourteen? What was happening in your life then?

What are you focusing on at work at the moment? Any annoying colleagues?

We're not just firing off random questions. We're getting them to talk about what they enjoy, what is important to them, or what has mattered in their lives – rather than about what specifically appeals to us. It's a way of showing love because, even if only for a short while, we're prioritising their happiness. And what may happen is that we discover the true commonalities of existence. Around the unalluring details of their lives all the deeper themes emerge: rivalries, disappointments, anxious hopes, fears, limitations, yearnings, small pleasures, unexpected happiness.

It is often only through our families that we have this strangely important opportunity: to be close to people whose characters don't intuitively appeal to us, to get to know the reality of lives lived by values other than our own. And we may find that we in return are loved by these individuals who in any other setting we would, very understandably but with great injustice, dismiss merely as bores and eccentrics.

YOU HAVE TO DO YOUR HOMEWORK

YOU HAVE TO DO YOUR HOMEWORK

One of the duties of parenthood is having to induct our beloved child into the reality – and horrors – of existence. Starting with homework.

It's been a difficult evening. Your 10-year-old was screaming that she wasn't going to do maths and your gentle encouragement didn't do any good. She kept asking 'why do I have to do it?' Now, as you say good night, you try to give her a proper answer.

$\longrightarrow$ *I know you'd rather not do it, and it's true that as an adult you'll probably never need to work out 6,397 divided by 82. You'll just use your phone (or whatever technology has replaced it). But sadly you're not being asked to do this because it's useful. You're being asked in order to introduce you to the idea that life is filled with things you have to do not because you want to but because you have to.*

Your child has drifted off to sleep but you keep talking, very quietly.

$\longrightarrow$ *The truth is, it will be like this again and again. You'll have to do so much you don't see the point of to get through this painful life. One day, many years from now, it will be 3pm on a Tuesday afternoon and it'll be lovely outside but you'll have to be analysing trends in electricity pricing in Belgium or chasing up a client who is deciding whether to invest in a multi-storey car park in Croydon. It won't interest you in the least, but you'll have to do it, because you'll have bills to pay and a career to uphold. You think homework will end when you finish school, but here's the truth: having to do things you don't want to do goes on throughout your life. It is – in many ways – what life is.*

When you are in a relationship, you'll need to do things your partner wants, even though they have no appeal for you. You'll have to visit their family; think of interesting things to say to their father about a film you didn't enjoy; make breezy conversation with their aunt who rather frightens you, or their brother, who you find entirely dull.

The agony will go on across a range of areas. Certain people will judge you in ways that are manifestly unfair, and you won't be able to do anything about it. Enemies will hate you for no reason. If you complain, you will be called thin-skinned.

You'll keep on thinking for a while that you can escape. Perhaps after university, or after you make some money, or once you're married, or after you get divorced, or once the children have left home. You'll dream of a place and time without anxiety, suffering and feelings of loss and alarm.

But you will never get there. All the while, you'll need to keep making enormous efforts and the fun times will get ever fewer and far between. You'll have to watch what you eat, even when you're longing to have another piece of carrot cake. You'll find that the most delicious things are fattening, and that at points in your life, you'll crave food as the only pleasure that you're allowed.

In your leisure time, you'll have to make yourself do stretching exercises because your limbs will start to stiffen.

One day, you'll notice how much you have aged. The bad photo of you from ten years back will exceed this year's most flattering shot.

There'll come a time when you'll have to force yourself to make an appointment to see the radiologist; you'll have to accept the dreadful verdict though it will obviously be idiotic that your life, your dazzling inner existence, your sheer loveliness and beauty and your delight in seeing the sky and the trees will all come to an end in this senseless, strange, amazing and exhilarating world.

Your life will in certain ways be a long sequence of different kinds of homework. Horribly, maths is the easiest version: a beginners' guide and almost a pleasure.

Poor darling. I love you more than I can say.

You turn the light down, move softly out of the room and head back to the kitchen, where your partner is wondering why you've been taking so long and keeping your child up too late when there's school in the morning – and where your laptop and the spreadsheets are waiting for you, open on the table.

THERE'S A FLY IN MY SOUP

THERE'S A FLY IN MY SOUP

In every life, we are constantly confronted with situations where a stranger will do something acutely irritating or discomforting: perhaps they'll turn up their music too loudly on the train, or they'll be wiggling their leg maddeningly next to us on the plane. Maybe they'll assign us a room in a hotel that has a strange musty smell or where a high-pitched whine is coming out of the air conditioning. In a restaurant, we may be given the worst table by the toilets, the bread may be stale and, proverbially, a fly may be found floating in the soup.

For many of us, our upbringing and cultural traditions will prepare us to say nothing at all in relation to these frustrations, and to forgive and overlook our agony instead. We may have emerged from childhood with a deep sense that we must – whatever happens – stay quiet and not cause a fuss for other people.

At the same time, we may inwardly twitch and boil. At points, we might even explode into sudden unpredictable rage. Though normally shy, we might surprise ourselves with the unbounded fury we let loose at the car rental desk, the hotel reception and with the hooded teenager in the train.

But neither the silence nor the rage seem, on reflection, to be quite the way forward. What we're ideally searching for is a way to be at once polite and honest, or civil and forthright.

To achieve this, we should – first and foremost – build up a good relationship with our own needs. This involves accepting that not everything that makes us happy will please others or be honoured as especially convenient – but that it can be important to explore and hold on to what we want nevertheless. The desire to be unfussy is one of the loveliest things in the world, but in order to have a genuinely good life, we may sometimes need to be (by the standards of the good child we once were) fruitfully and bravely a bit tricky.

At the same time, in order not to shout, we must hold on, even in very challenging situations, to a distinction between what someone does – and what they may have meant to do. Our idea of motives is crucial. Unfortunately, we're seldom very good at perceiving what motives really happen to be involved in the incidents that drive us mad. We are easily and wildly mistaken. We see intention where there was none and escalate and confront when no strenuous or agitated response is warranted.

Part of the reason why we jump so readily to dark conclusions and therefore shout more than we should, is a rather poignant psychological phenomenon: self-hatred. The less we like ourselves, the more we appear in our own eyes as really rather plausible targets for mockery and harm. Why would a drill have started up outside, just as we were settling down to work? Why is the room service breakfast not arriving, even though we will have to be in a meeting very soon? Why would the phone operator be taking so long to find our details? Because there is – logically enough – a plot against us. Because we are appropriate targets for these kinds of things, because we are the sort of people against whom disruptive drilling is legitimately likely to be directed: because it's what we deserve. When we carry an excess of self-disgust around with us, operating just below the radar of conscious awareness, we'll constantly seek confirmation from the wider world that we really are the worthless people we take ourselves to be.

The ideal complaint emerges from an unparanoid assumption: they aren't deliberately setting out to irritate us; they haven't got a plan to make us unhappy; they really just haven't thought about us very much at all. We're able to imagine that they could be quite a nice and reasonable person who nevertheless – without thinking about it – has upset us profoundly.

$\longrightarrow$ *Sorry to be a bore, I'm sure you don't realise but the back of your seat is squashing against my knees.*

Apologies for interrupting, I can't help overhearing more of your conversation than I should.

I rather love this song as well, but at the moment, I need to get some sleep.

I know it's not your fault, but a fly does seem to have entangled itself in the minestrone.

The actual words hardly matter, what counts is the lightness of tone that comes from an impression of the legitimacy of one's position and of the likely innocence of those who annoy us most. Viewed in this way, complaining is not an insult, it's an ambitious, authentic and ultimately kind attempt to offer someone a minor piece of education.

The School of Life: Quotes to Live By

A collection to revive and inspire

**A collection of enlightening quotes to deliver some of
the most important lessons The School of Life has to offer,
accompanied by humorous illustrations.**

This is a selection of the very best and most psychologically
acute quotations from The School of Life, covering such large
and diverse topics as relationships, regret, anxiety, work, friends,
family, travel and, not least, the meaning of life. Some of these
quotations elicit an immediate nod of recognition, others leave
us thoughtful – and a few are just plain funny.

Together, this collection of quotes amounts to a tour around the
most profound sorrows and joys of the human mind and heart
– in a compact format ideally suited to our impatient, anxious,
searching times.

ISBN: 978-1-915087-04-1
£15 | $19.99

The School of Life is a global organisation helping people lead more fulfilled lives. It is a resource for helping us understand ourselves, for improving our relationships, our careers and our social lives – as well as for helping us find calm and get more out of our leisure hours. We do this through films, workshops, books and gifts – and provide a warm and supportive community. You can find us online, in stores and in welcoming spaces around the globe.